My Amazing Toddler
Behavioral Series

I Sing and Clap.
I Don't WORRY!

An Affirmation-Themed Toddler Book
About Worrying (Ages 2-4)

By Suzanne T. Christian

TWORAVENS
B O O K S

Two Little Ravens
CHILDREN'S NON-FICTION BOOKS

Paperback Edition: 9781964202891
Hardcover Edition: 9781964202907
Digital Edition: 9781964202914

Published in the United States by Two Ravens Books LLC,
254 Chapman Rd, Ste 209, Newark DE 19702

'Expand the mind, free the imagination, one title at a time.'
www.tworavensbooks.com

Welcome to
"I Sing and Clap.
I Don't Worry!"

This book is a playful collection of simple affirmations created just for toddlers. As you read together, your child will learn that feeling worried is normal and that worries don't stay forever.

With catchy phrases, upbeat rhythms, and familiar daily experiences, young children are able to deal with usual worries, including loud sounds, trips to the doctor, mishaps on the potty, and night shadows at bed-time. Singing, clapping, and giggling make large worries smaller ones, and little ones feel safe and brave.

This charming book exposes your toddler to relaxing stress-busting strategies, developing resilience and calm feelings. Repeated reading of this book not only consolidates their learning, but also provides confidence building, calmness, and secure attachment for both of you.

Enjoy reading together!

Suzanne T. Christian

When I feel a worry
in my tummy,
I sing, I laugh, I play.

Everyone feels worried sometimes, but worries don't stay forever; they float away.

My grown-up waves bye-bye,
but always comes back!

When I meet my new teacher, I wave and say, **"Hello, hello!"** I don't worry!

When I meet a new friend,
I smile and say, **"Hi!"**

Boom goes the thunder,
I say, **"Hello thunder,"**
and **"BOOM"** right back!

The vacuum says
vroom vroom,
I roar even louder!
I don't worry!

Fireworks go bang
bang, I say,
"Hooray! I am brave!"

When I need to pee
or poop, I say,
"Potty time!" and
do my potty dance.

If I miss the potty, I giggle and say, **'No worries, I'll try again!'**

Dogs bark loudly; it's how they say hello! I go **woof woof** too, silly me!

Sometimes the doctor gives a tiny pinch, then it's all done! I don't worry!

When I hold my grown-up's hand at the store,
I feel safe, no worries!

When I see shadows in the dark, I laugh and say, 'Silly shadow!'

I know monsters are not real, they are just pretend! I don't worry!

When it's time for bed,
I say, "Nighty-night."
I feel safe.

My grown-up keeps
me safe every day.
I don't worry!

I Sing and Clap.

I Don't WORRY!

The End!

My Amazing Toddler Behavioral Series

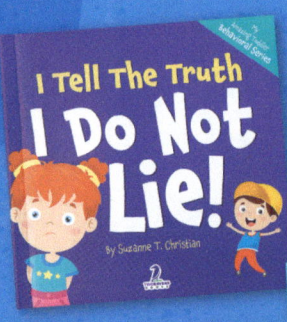

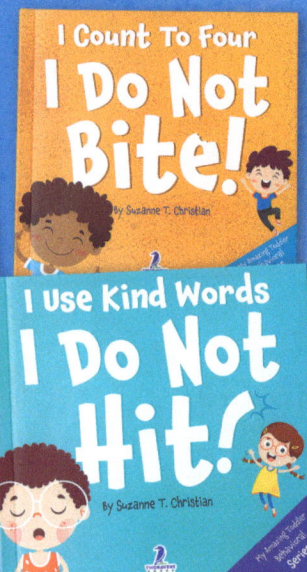

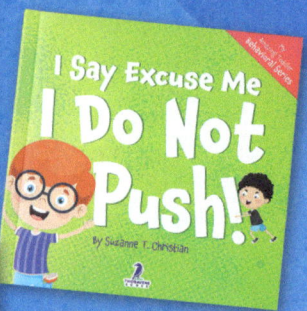

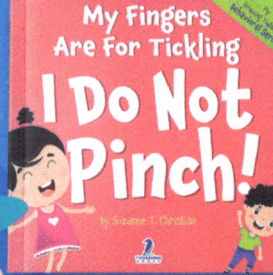

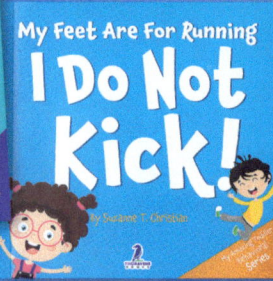

Check Out
Suzanne T. Christian's beloved series
'My Amazing Toddler Behavioral Series'.
Young readers are sure to enjoy!

Two Little Ravens

CHILDREN'S NON-FICTION BOOKS

Dear Amazing Reader,

Thank you for diving into **I Sing and Clap. I Don't Worry!** with me. If this book touched your heart or made a difference for a young reader, I'd be grateful if you could share your thoughts in a review. Your feedback inspires my future work and helps others discover the magic within these pages.

I'd love to hear from you directly if you have suggestions or ideas for improving the book. Please feel free to reach out to me at **suzanne.christian@tworavensbooks.com.** Your voice counts, and I cherish it deeply.

With heartfelt gratitude,